The Adventures and Blunders of Hannah Hucklebee

The Adventures and Blunders of Hannah Hucklebee

Barbara F Barnett

This book is dedicated to the **Victims and Survivors of September 27, 2024 Hurricane Helene** that flooded and destroyed many homes as well as took untold numbers of lives in **Old Fort and surrounding areas.** May you always remain
MOUNTAIN STRONG

I also dedicate this book to **Old Fort Elementary School.** It is with fond memories and love that I pray you will soon be up and running again and loving the children as much as you loved me when I was a child.

Love in Christ,

Barbara Lewis Barnett

Copyright © 2025 by Barbara Barnett
All rights reserved. No part of this book may be reproduced in any manner whatsoever without written permission except in the case of brief quotations embodied in critical articles and reviews.
First Printing, 2025

Contents

Dedication **iii**

2 Hannah Hucklebee **2**

4 Hannah Hucklebee and the Jump **7**

6 Hannah Hucklebee and the Girl Scout Trip **12**

8 Hannah Hucklebee and the Thunderstorm **17**

10 Hannah Hucklebee and The Hiding Place **21**

12 Hannah Hucklebee and the Mud Turtle **26**

14 Hannah Hucklebee Becomes A Song Writer **32**

16 Hannah Hucklebee and the Apple Tree **36**

17 Hurricane Helene Intro **40**

19 Hannah Hucklebee and the Great Flood **43**

About the Author **50**
Acknowledgements and Citations **51**

{ **1** }

The Birthday Party

{ 2 }

Hannah Hucklebee

Hannah Hucklebee turned ten years old this week. Her mother had planned for a birthday celebration on Saturday in the small town of Old Fort, North Carolina. The year was 1969.

She had been waiting for an entire year to reach the double numbers. She was no longer considered a little girl. Her birthday cake had been decided on as strawberry with strawberry icing. Balloons were strung along the living room with streamers hanging from the ceiling. Ice cream waited in the freezer for the big event. Potato chips topped off the menu. All her friends were invited. Even Freddie, her best friend and cousin.

Hannah was thinking of her father. She always called him "Daddy". He was the best dad in the world to Hannah. Unfortunately, her father had passed away a year ago from a car wreck. She had been terribly hurt when learning of his passing. It left her mother, Martha, raising Hannah and her other siblings alone. She had three sisters and two brothers. Linda was the oldest then, Nina, Teddy, Donna and Chester.

Her mother worked as a schoolteacher at the elementary school in town. She loved being a teacher and was exceptionally good at her job. She often would say that education was important, and she hoped her children would go to school and make a change in the world. Hannah wanted to grow up to be a teacher like her mom.

Mom told Hannah it would be nice if she would wear one of her dresses to the party. Hannah hated the idea of putting on a dress, especially on a Saturday when she would normally wear shorts and a tee shirt. She was an adventurous child at heart, and she loved playing in the dirt and wrestling with Freddie. Her hair was strawberry blond, almost red, and hung on her shoulders in ringlets. Hannah also had freckles on her face that showed more in the summer when she would get a sun tan from playing outside in the sun.

Freddie, her cousin, was two months younger than Hannah. He was tall and lanky with brown hair. He had been Hannah's friend as long as she could remember. They did everything together from going to school to going to church. Often, they would camp out in the back yard of Freddie's house in a tent after cooking hot dogs on an open fire under Freddie's dad, Bill's, supervision. Bill was brother to Hannah's father.

On this day, Hannah was in her bedroom trying to figure out if she could fit her shorts under her dress. Her mom had made Hannah a beautiful dress of light blue dotted Swiss with tiny white dots all over the fabric. It had short sleeves that were puffy and tied at the back with a blue ribbon. She wore a crinoline slip with it that made it poof out. The dress was usually worn for Sunday church services with a pair of black shiny shoes and turned down white socks with lace trim.

Freddie finally arrived before the other guests and to Hannah's disbelief wore a pair of black pants with a plaid shirt that buttoned all the way down the front. Hannah giggled at Freddie who blushed and stuck his tongue out at her. He stated, "You don't look much better with your hair all pinned up and in a dress." Hannah had to agree, but she still giggled at him.

Other guests started to arrive. Each carried a present of puzzles, bubbles, books or bracelets. A game of pin the tale on the donkey was started. The children played Bum-Bum-Bum and tag with screams and laughter ringing throughout the yard. The mothers all sat on the front porch talking about local gossip. Freddie was called down by his mother for pushing Hannah down, but Hannah didn't mind. It was part of the game. Finally, the time came to cut the cake. And with a rousing rendition of "Happy Birthday to You" and candles blown out, the party ended.

With fond farewells, all the children left with their parents. The party was over and Hannah, tired from the day's event, took off the blue dress and hung it in the closet. Slipping on her shorts and tee shirt Hannah lay down on the bed in her room thinking of the wonderful time of the day. Hannah thought the only thing that was missing was her daddy. But she knew he was in heaven watching the party with a big smile. Slowly her eyes closed, and sleep came softly as it always did to a young girl of ten.

{ 5 } ~ BARBARA F BARNETT

{ 3 }

The Big Jump

Ready for the Big Jump

{ 4 }

Hannah Hucklebee and the Jump

Hannah Hucklebee sat astride her bicycle with the fierceness of a warrior as she eyed the wooden ramp at the foot of the driveway. Her hands tightened on the handlebars as she prepared for the descent down the driveway, over the ramp and across the three rubber tires she and her cousin, Freddie, had lined up side by side. Her fear was outweighed only by her determination to prove to Freddie that she was the bravest of the two of them and that she would out jump him to day. Bragging rights were on the line. Also, her bike was on the line because she had told Freddie she was willing to bet the bicycle against his baseball and glove if she lost.

Hannah was the older of the two cousins by three months. With reddish-blonde hair and a tom boyish spirit she felt she had to out do Freddie in almost all physical games. Freddie was a good cousin except for being boastful of his achievements at school and in sports.

Hannah envied Freddie too, after losing her own father in a car wreck a year ago. She envied that he had a father, her Uncle Bill, who was her father's brother. Although she had a wonderful mom who took care of her, Hannah still missed having a father to go fishing with and stand up for her when she needed one.

She looked at the length of the driveway and considered that it might not be enough to get the momentum to take flight over the tires. Never the less she was determined today was the day to stop all the jokes Freddie had been making for the past week. His last remark was, "You are such a girlie girl. There is no way you can out do me on a bicycle." Of all the things to say to her, that was the worst.

As she began her descent, the gravel crackled beneath the tires of the bicycle. The wind picked up the tendrils of her hair as her speed continued to increase. Freddie began running down the hill behind Hannah as she gripped the handlebars tighter. From the kitchen window her mother looked in awe at the spectacle before her. Throwing her hand towel into the sink she ran through the kitchen yelling Hannah's name.

Just as Hannah approached the wooden ramp, made from two by four planks, there appeared from her side vision the most disturbing sight. Molly, Hannah's gray and black Persian cat, ran from the front porch being chased by Freddie's German Shepherd dog, Hobo. Their direction seemed to be straight for the tires Hannah was intending to careen over.

Hannah quickly recalculated her arrival at the ramp and reconsidered her decision to outdo her cousin. Thinking she had only a second to respond, Hannah turned her bicycle handles to the left and veered off the runway heading to the tall grass beside the driveway. Hannah flew up and over the handrails hitting the grass.

Freddie ran to Hannah's side helping her to stand just as her mother ran from the kitchen doorway. The look of terror was replaced with a sigh of relief from Martha's lips. Hannah stood, legs wobbling, her face white as if she had seen a ghost. The first thing she thought to do was to hug Freddie. He staggered backwards with a look of shock on his face. He pushed Hannah away stating "Ugh...what's the big idea!"

Hannah stepped back and cleared her throat. "Did you see that wreck?" she kidded, as she turned to pick up her bike. Unable to admit she was so happy to have a great cousin like Freddie to be by her side in an emergency. She forgot all the times Freddie had bragged about his accomplishments thankful he was there to pick her up when she fell.

Hannah's mom looked at the scene of the two cousins and realized she was watching a lasting friendship being made. Although Hannah had been having a hard time since her father's death, today she appeared to be accepting of the love she had around her. Times had been hard since his passing but today Hannah's mom felt the first feelings of things going well. She turned and walked back into the house, foregoing a lecture for the daredevil stunt she had just witnessed.

Hannah and Freddie, along with the cat and dog, walked over to the ramp and began taking it apart." That would have been a great jump if you had made it" Freddie said. Hannah looked at him and smiled. "Yeah, it would have, wouldn't it? But I bet I drove down the driveway faster than you!"

They both laughed as they rolled the tires to the back of the house. Having a friend was a lot better than competing with them.

{ 5 }

Chased by Dogs

Being Chased by the Dogs

{ 6 }

Hannah Hucklebee and the Girl Scout Trip

The summer sun was playing over the grass as white, billowy clouds rolled over the morning sky. Hannah was up early this morning and already out in the front yard checking the tires on her bicycle and oiling the chain with lubricant. She had been looking forward to this Saturday for several days since learning of the first Girl Scout adventure of the summer.

At the last meeting of the scouts on Tuesday, Hannah had found out that the troop leaders were taking ten girls of troop 114, Old Fort division, on a bicycle ride from the local church to the golf course. They would have a bagged lunch and then return after visiting the nearby golf course.

Everyone was excited for the trip, but Hannah was a little apprehensive because she had only recently learned how to ride without training wheels. She had been practicing every day this week after school but was still having trouble with stopping the bike. Also, her bike was not as big as the other girl's bicycles. But that was not going to stop Hannah from the outing of a lifetime. Hannah was not sure how far the ride was to the golf course, but she estimated at least five miles. She felt this was a big step up from being a little girl and would secure her a place in the Girl Scout Troop and show her leaders how big she really was.

Finally, the time came to meet the other scouts at the church. Mom had prepared her a peanut butter and jelly sandwich wrapped in wax paper. She had also placed a bag of chips and a Coca-Cola in a can in the bag topping it off with three chocolate chip cookies. It was a young girls feast for a momentous day.

The troop leaders explained to the scouts they would be riding in a single line. The girls were also refreshed on bicycle hand signals for the turns and road changes to the golf course. "Safety was the key issue" the leaders said. One troop leader would be in the front, one in the middle and the last in the rear with the slower peddlers. Hannah was determined to be at least in the middle if not in the front.

After everyone was prepared for the safety of the trip, off they started. The trip was exciting during the first mile or two. But by the time they reached the golf course, Hannah felt as if her legs would fall off right on the ground. She did not want to complain though because she thought it would be a sign of being a big baby. So, Hannah sucked in her breath and acted as if she could walk normally all the time her legs were screaming, "What are you walking for, fall down!".

Finally, the troop leaders told the girls to sit down and rest for awhile and enjoy their bagged lunch. Hannah ate her picnic lunch with the other girls. some of them complained about the ride and how sore their legs were but not Hannah. She just replied, "Oh it was no big deal. I could have ridden another mile or two."

After visiting the golf course and going to the restroom, the time came to ride back to the church. The girls began gathering their bicycles for the long ride back the same way they had come. Fortunately for Hannah the ride back was mostly downhill. It was near the turn off to the church that things began to get interesting.

Hannah was making good speed down one particular neighborhood when out of a neighbor's yard ran three big dogs. The dogs, one black, one white and one spotted ran after the bicycles. They were barking so loudly that Hannah did not know how to react. All she could think of was how little her bicycle was and how big the dogs were. Fearing for her life, Hannah placed her feet onto the handlebars of the bike and closed her eyes hoping for the best as she flew at breakneck speed down the road, around the curve and onto the turn off road to the church.

The sound of the dogs slowly vanished but Hannah kept going. She sped past the church and down her driveway. In all the excitement she forgot how to use the brakes. Hannah pointed the front of the tires toward her front porch. Slamming her feet down on the brake pedals she ran into the porch and fell over onto the ground.

Mom ran outside to see what the crashing sound and screams were about and found Hannah lying on her back looking up at those same billowy clouds. Her mother picked her up and asked her if she was okay. Hannah, taking a deep breath, turned to her , and said, "Yeah, I am okay. But Mom, the next time the Girl Scouts go on a trip...I sure hope they take a bus!".

{ 15 } ~ BARBARA F BARNETT

{ 7 }

The Storm

Hannah is Terrified of Lightning

{ 8 }

Hannah Hucklebee and the Thunderstorm

The air had been very warm on this Monday afternoon. A light breeze blew through the trees near Hannah's home. Teddy and Chester were in the woods playing cowboys as usual and Linda, Nina and Donna were in the house cleaning the bedroom. Mom had called from town that she would be a little late getting home so she had instructed each of the children to do their chores.

Teddy and Chester had finished taking out the trash and picking up the bicycles from the yard with the other toys. Hannah was instructed to sweep the front and back porches and bring in the laundry from the clothesline. She had accomplished this feat but there were many clothespins lying on the ground after jerking the clothes off the line and shoving them in a basket.

The wind appeared to be picking up a little bit as the family car came down the driveway. Hannah was struggling with the clothes basket when Teddy, who was stronger, came from behind and helped her with her burden. Chester picked up the stray clothespins and started pinching Teddy on the back of the arms with them. Teddy dropped the basket and took off running after him.

Suddenly, a flash of lightning streaked across the sky. Mom jumped out of the car and yelled for the trio to get in the house. Rain started to come from the clouds above as Hannah, who loved rain showers, ran to the front porch to watch. Mom ran to the side of the house and grabbed the television antenna and with all her strength hoisted the antenna off the bank at the side of the house. She then ran inside and had all the kids cut off the lights in the house and climb up on the bed.

Hannah's mom, Martha, had been afraid of thunderstorms from a young age. She thought of television antennas as lightning rods and feared a strike would hit the house. Hannah, too, was terrified of lightning storms and crawled up closer to her mom on the bed. The other kids became quiet as the storm rolled over the house.

As suddenly as it began, the storm passed by. Mom helped each of the children off the bed and began turning lights on again. Warm light flooded the house as Hannah rushed to the living room window to see if the rain had caused a stream down the driveway as usual.

It was nearly six o'clock by this time and the best television shows were about to come on the set. But the television antenna was still off in the weeds beside the driveway. With the help of the boys, Mom was able to get the antenna back in the ground beside the chimney. After hooking the line back to the T.V. set, Teddy turned the antenna pointing it in the correct position for signal. Linda, Nina and Donna yelled instructions from the living room as the antenna was pointed north, south, east and west. Finally, Linda yelled, "Hold it right there. That's it!" as the channel became clear enough to see shows like "The Lone Ranger" and "Wild Wild West."

Dinner was completed and all the kids sat in the floor or on the couch to watch the shows. Mom took her place in the rocking chair with her sewing in hand.

Hannah looked on as the television shows announcer stated, "We will be back after a word from our sponsor." Mom, realizing the lateness of the hour stood and ordered everyone to start getting ready for bed.

With sounds of disappointment each of the children headed for bed. But Hannah stopped long enough to look out of the window to see lightning in the far distance. One day she hoped she and her mother would no longer fear the storms but ride them out together.

{ 19 } ~ BARBARA F BARNETT

{ 9 }

The Hiding Place

{ 10 }

Hannah Hucklebee and The Hiding Place

Hannah had the day to play while mom graded test papers. Her other sisters were either watching television or reading a book, Her two brothers were playing cowboys in the woods beside the house. They were going about their day having fun on their own.

Hannah, feeling lonely today, had asked each of her siblings if they would like to play with her. She would have asked her cousin , Freddie, but he had a toothache and had to go to the dentist. No one wanted to play. She walked around the house a couple of times and thought about riding her bike up and down the driveway but did not want to ride her bicycle to day.

After a few more laps walking around the house Hannah began wondering if they even loved her. After all she was a middle child and often she felt she was left out. Her two older sisters talked and giggled together. Her brothers played together, and her younger sister read books all the time. She began to feel sorry for herself as the morning wore on.

"I bet they wouldn't miss me if I disappeared from the face of the earth!" Hannah thought. This thought began to take root in her brain as Hannah kicked a rock from the gravel drive. Gradually a plan began to form in Hannah's mind.

While the television played the latest show of "The Monkees" Hannah slipped into the living room and hid behind the plastic curtains facing the driveway. Mom had bought the plastic curtains in a floral design from the local merchandise store with the intention of updating the living room. Hannah stood quietly behind the curtain hiding from her brothers and sisters.

"I'll teach them not to play with me." She thought. Hannah, although usually a good girl, was hurt by being ignored by her siblings. "I'll hide here all day if I have to."

After an hour of standing behind the curtain, the television show ended, and her sisters started yelling out for Hannah. Being a stubborn girl, Hannah smiled but did not say a word. The sisters continued to call out, but Hannah was resolved to keep silent.

Her sisters ran outside and asked the two brothers if they had seen Hannah. And after a quick "No!" they all ran inside to ask Donna, the younger sister. Still a firm "No!" was the answer as she joined in the posse'. The only choice they had was to go to their mother to report Hannah was missing.

Hannah then realized that things were getting serious when her mother joined in the search. She did not want to worry her mother. She just wanted to scare her siblings. She did not think her siblings would go so far as to include their mom in the search. But by this time Hannah was in over her head and feared the punishment she might receive for hiding so long.

As the search continued, Hannah thought of trying to open the window behind her and sneak out, but she was too far from the ground and was afraid someone would see the curtain move as she made her escape. Fear clutched her heart as suddenly her sister , Nina, yelled "I've found her! She's behind the curtain!".

Yanking back the curtain, Nina stood looking at Hannah along with the entire family. "Have you been hiding behind here the whole time we were looking for you?" Nina shouted. She was joined by all the other siblings with questions of the same.

"Oh, Hannah, I have been worried sick. Didn't you hear us call for you?" Mom said holding Hannah by the shoulders as tears ran down her face. "I thought something bad had happened to you."

Hannah was embarrassed at the whole scene. She certainly did not think they would all react like this. She did not want to worry her mother. Her prank had gotten out of control before she realized what she had done.

"I didn't think anyone loved me because they wouldn't play with me" Hannah told her mom. "Boy you are a big dummy" her brother Teddy said. "Yeah" echoed Chester as they went back outside.

"I'm sorry Mom" Hannah said. "I just thought nobody cared for me." Her mom hugged her and stated, "Hannah, your whole family loves you a great deal. You are incredibly special, and no one could take your place in this family. But, because you hid from us, there is no television for you tonight. Instead, you must help me fix dinner."

Somehow this sounded fun to Hannah as she made her way to the kitchen to help. Hannah thought how great it was to be in a family that genuinely loved her even though they might not play with you.

Spending time with Mom and helping fix dinner turned out to be more fun than punishment. They fixed hot dogs with chili and corn cheese with grape Kool-Aid. That was Hannah's favorite. The day ended a lot better than it started. Hannah realized sometimes it was not so bad being the middle child after all.

{ 11 }

Fishing at Wildlife Lake

Hannah and Freddie Fishing at the Pond

{ 12 }

Hannah Hucklebee and the Mud Turtle

Hannah and Freddie were up early Saturday morning. They were going fishing at the nearby wildlife lake. Often neighbors would take the short walk down to the lake to fish for anything they could pull from the small pond near Hanna's house. It was not really a lake but a small pond that came from the nearby dairy farm past her church.

This made a little difference to Hannah and Freddie because to them it was a big lake filled with adventure. The walk to the lake was down the hill from their grandparents' house. She loved her grandparents and planned to take her catch of fish to their grandmother for a gift. All plans were to catch as many fish as she could carry, string them up and deliver her gift for a fish fry.

The sun was warm but not too hot. Freddie had a bag of cookies for a snack along with two bologna sandwiches his mother had placed in a paper bag. They found a spot near a tree and set up two sticks with a V-shape cut in the ends to prop the fishing poles on. After casting their lines into the water, Hannah and Freddie leaned back against a tree to wait for the first catch of the day.

Time slipped on slowly with no bites at all. Freddie thought he had a massive fish on his line at one time but it ended up being a shoe someone had tossed into the water. As time slowly drifted on by, with no fish to be had, suddenly there was a wiggle on Hannah's line. Freddie nudged Hannah who had almost dozed off and pointed to the fishing pole as it bent over. Hannah jumped up and grabbed the fishing pole as it was yanked off the stick grabbing it just as it was about to be pulled into the lake.

"It's a big one!" Freddie yelled as their excitement grew. "Don't let it get away!"

Hannah was breathless as she began reeling in the monstrous fish on the other end of the line. She thought how happy her grandmother would be to have a huge fish to fix for her grandfather. Her arms were getting weaker as the fight with the giant fish continued. It took what seemed like an hour before Hannah and Freddie were able to see what was on the other end of the line.

As they drew the line closer, Hannah realized that her gigantic fish was, to her surprise, a brown, slimy mud turtle. Freddie started laughing and fell on the ground holding his stomach. "It's a dang mud turtle!" he snorted. Hannah pulled the mud turtle onto the bank and sat down beside Freddie. " A mud turtle? What are we going to do with a mud turtle?" she replied.

Knowing mud turtles were able to bite, Hannah stated "I heard that if you get bit by a mud turtle, they won't let go until it thunders." Freddie said, "Yeah, so what do we do?" Hannah thought for a moment and shouted, "I know. We'll have it bite on a stick, that way it can't bite us."

Thinking they were very smart indeed, and the problem was solved, Freddie picked up a stick and sure enough the mud turtle bit into the stick and would not let go. "Now what do we do with it?" he questioned.

Noticing the day was about to be over and it was time to go home, Hannah came up with another idea. Since they had not caught the great fish supper Hannah had expected, she decided on Plan B. "We'll take it to my grandparents anyway. They need a pet, and this will make a fine pet, but they will have to wait until it thunders to get the stick out of his mouth." Freddie, holding the dangling turtle in the air stated, "Sounds good to me."

After eating their sandwiches and packing up their fishing poles, Hannah and Freddie headed back up the hill toward their grandparents' house, stick and mud turtle in hand. Hannah was so excited to be bringing this gift to her grandparents and was thinking how surprised her grandmother would be to have a pet turtle.

Arriving at their destination, Hannah instructed Freddie to wait outside while she fetched her grandmother. Freddie waited as ordered, stick in hand with the mud turtle hanging on for dear life. Hannah ran to the back of the house with the screen door slamming as she ran through. "Grandma come quick. We have a surprise for you."

"What is it you want young'un?" Grandma answered. "And what's the big hurry?"

Grandma came from the kitchen wiping her hands on her apron from washing dishes. "What kind of surprise?" she said. Hannah replied, "Wait till you see. Now close your eyes and I will lead you. Don't look until I tell you to!"

Hannah's grandmother was used to her grandchildren's surprises but played along to please Hannah. Slowly they made their way from the kitchen and off the back porch to the back yard.

"Now open your eyes!" Hannah said anxiously. She knew her grandmother was going to be so excited. Grandmother opened her eyes and to her amazement, there stood Freddie, holding a stick in his hand with a squirming, pitiful mud turtle dangling helplessly in the air.

"Surprise!" Hannah yelled. Grandmother could not believe her eyes. This was not what she was expecting. Seeing the proud look on the children's faces though, Grandmother put her hand over her mouth and stated. "I have never seen such a fine mud turtle in my life. Where on earth did you catch such an amazing turtle?"

Hannah and Freddie retold the entire story, leaving out the shoe Freddie caught. Grandmother, understanding the excitement and love the turtle had brought to the children came up with a plan of her own. "You know it would be a shame to take this turtle away from its family. I bet they are down there in the pond wondering where he is right now. But I can go get a cage down in the basement." As she turned she added "But his little children might be down there in the pond crying for their daddy."

Hannah and Freddie had not thought of the family of the turtle. They had been so caught up with their surprise they had forgotten that he might have a family too.

"Grandma, if you will let us take this turtle back to his family, we will get you another gift later on. Would that be okay with you?" Grandmother stepped back and said, "Why kids that is a great idea. I hadn't thought of that." She hugged both Hannah and Freddie for the gift of love they had shown.

As the two kids walked away down the hill and toward the pond, Freddie still holding the turtle attached to the stick., Grandma thought to herself, "I love those two kids but, Lord help me , what was I going to do with a mud turtle?"

{ 13 }

Singing in School

Singing her Song in School

{ 14 }

Hannah Hucklebee Becomes A Song Writer

Hannah Hucklebee was headed into her fourth grade classroom feeling tired but excited. She had spent the last night writing a song. She had never written a song before but for the past two or three days some words kept going over in her head. She loved her English studies and liked writing poems. But the song that was running through her mind was special to Hannah.

On Sundays, Hannah and her mother along with her other siblings would go to church. She loved singing in the choir and dreamed of someday writing her own gospel song. She loved the old songs they sang in choir. She wondered what Heaven's choir would sound like.

Last night after Hannah had completed her homework, she sat at the kitchen table thinking of verses and a tune for her first gospel song. As she considered how beautiful Heaven would be, Hannah thought it was important to tell everyone she could how much Jesus loved them. Hannah wrote the following words:

> My God is your God. He knows every move you make.
> He's up in Heaven, making a home, where I will stay.
> He's building a mansion, way up in the sky, way up on high.
> I will go up to Heaven to live by and by.

The words were simple but seemed expertly put together by Hannah. She thought she had expressed what she felt was important to tell everyone.

The next step Hannah decided was to give the song verse to her school music teacher. She would ask her to add music to the verse. Ms. Gibbs was a small, framed woman but had a big voice. She helped the children with vocals as well as the school band. Hannah was not aware, though, the Ms. Gibbs would ask Hannah to stand before the whole class and teach them the song.

The class was going to the auditorium after lunch for music lessons. As Hannah entered the front of the group, Ms. Gibbs pulled her aside and gave her copies of the song she had printed off earlier that day. After passing out the sheet of paper to her classmates, Hannah stood beside the piano as Ms. Gibbs took her seat and began playing a tune Hannah was not familiar with. But she was going to try her best to make her song sound as angelic as those she had heard in church.

Unfortunately, as all the children, looked at Hannah, stage fright set in and Hannah found she could hardly breathe, much less sing. After a few attempts to sing the song, the classroom caught on and Hannah became more confident that everything was going to be okay. Time after time they repeated the song and the tune until Hannah felt it was good enough to pass. Ms. Gibbs was glad the other children were taking part in the music class and attempting to compose songs and sing.

Hannah got back to her class and thought to herself that she was so scared she would never write another song in her life. Even though she had managed to get through the song and was excited about the outcome, she did not know if her nerves could stand being in front of a whole classroom of kids as she was today.

As Hannah returned home later that day and was preparing for bed, she knelt beside her bed and thanked God for helping her write her first song. Hannah prayed, "Dear Lord, thank you for giving me a song to write. I know it might not have been as good as the songs in church, but I hope you enjoyed it."

Deep in Hannah's heart she felt like God was pleased with her song and was sitting in Heaven with her Daddy and they both had a big smile on their faces.

{ 15 }

Apple Trees and Injuries

Snitching Apples

{ 16 }

Hannah Hucklebee and the Apple Tree

    Sunday school at church was one of the best things Hannah Hucklebee liked. She loved her Sunday school teacher, Mrs. Myrtle, and loved to learn new things from the Bible. Today's lesson was on David and Goliath, one of Hannah's most cherished stories. Often her daddy had read the story to her at home, and she felt as if she knew the story by heart. She always loved her times at night when daddy and mom would call her and her other brothers and sisters into the living room before bed. They would pray and sing songs before daddy read the Bible stories before bedtime.

    Those days were different though now since her father had passed away in a car crash last year. But Hannah still enjoyed coming to the family church and hearing the stories over again as if her daddy were telling them himself. Hannah was glad that she had been brought up in a home of love and joy. She was especially glad that her mother and father took her to church.

    Running upstairs to the sanctuary, Hannah and her cousin Freddie headed outside for a drink of water from the outside fountain. There was a fifteen minute intermission between Sunday school and preaching service and Hannah made use of this time to quench her thirst before service began. She had been told on several occasions to "Get a drink of water and go to the restroom because you are not getting up in church" by her mother. Most of the parents warned their children to behave in church or else "I'll take you downstairs." The children understood this to mean your bottom would get a tanning or worse.

Hannah had been also warned by her mother not to go to the house next door and snitch apples from the apple trees that sat on a hill beside the church. Those were the best apples Hannah and Freddie had ever eaten. They were sour and sweet and hard all at the same time. It made their mouths water just thinking about the apples and lunch time was still a little while off.

"I bet you and me could go over there and get an apple and be back in two shakes" whispered Freddie. "I dare you to go get one." Hannah hated being dared by anyone. He just as well said she was a chicken. Forgetting she was in a dress Hannah took that dare and slowly meandered toward the bank leading to the apple trees. She looked back over her shoulder at Freddie who was hiding between two cars in the parking lot. Forgetting that her mother had warned her to stay away from that bank, Hannah scrambled up the hill and grabbed two green apples.

Before she could get caught, she began her descent back down the hill hoping to jump the short distance to the parking lot of the church. Unknowing to her there was a piece of barbed wire hiding beneath the grass on the hillside. Before Hannah knew what was happening her foot became entangled in the barbed wire and she was falling face first onto the gravel of the road.

Freddie, seeing Hannah on the road, ran up to her to see if she was dead. Hannah raised her face to reveal blood and dirt trickling down her face. The apples were nowhere to be seen having rolled down the drive and off another hill.

Freddie began crying thinking Hannah was going to kick the bucket and that he was going to be grounded for the rest of his life. Running to the church in search of Hannah's mom Freddie dashed off. Hannah got up and staggered toward the church, scratched up but still on this side of Heaven.

Within a few minutes mom came running out of the church to find Hannah with a road rash on her forehead and torn tights on her legs. There were scrapes on her kneecaps and hands but overall she was none the worse for wear. The scared look on her face was more for having disobeyed her mother's warnings and now having to own up to her disobedience.

Hannah's mom took her to the water fountain and with a paper towel from Freddie cleansed the dirt from the wounds.

"I"m sorry mom" Hannah pleaded. "I should have listened to you." thinking the worse was still to come when she got home. Mom looked at Hannah and said, "I guess bad girls whoop themselves. I hope that apple was worth it."

"I don't know, it rolled down the hill." Hannah said in reply. Her mom turned her back to Hannah trying to muffle her giggles at the unfortunate pair. Turning she replied,"I guess you've been punished enough for disobeying."

Hannah, with tears in her eyes, looked at her mom and smiled faintly. "I guess I'll not be eating apples for a while." As they re-entered the church Freddie said,"They were probably wormy anyway." Hannah agreed as she limped into the church and sat on the church pew thinking to herself she had the best mom in the world.

{ 39 } ~ BARBARA F BARNETT

{ 17 }

Hurricane Helene Intro

The last story in this book is about Hurricane Helene, but is written as if it had happened in the 1960's. I lived through a flood in Old Fort, North Carolina, forty six years ago. And although devastating as it was, it was a spring shower compared to what happened on September 27th, 2024.

I hope you can feel an inkling of the sorrow I felt as I have driven through my hometown recently before publishing this book. I have prayed that God will bless the publishing and distribution of this first edition in the "Hannah Hucklebee" series so that I may give a percentage of the proceeds of this book to the rebuilding efforts in Old Fort.

God bless you and continue to pray for the flood victims and survivors of Hurricane Helene for it will be a long road to recovery.

Sincerely,
Barbara Barnett

{ 41 } ~ BARBARA F BARNETT

{ 18 }

High Waters and Destruction

Hannah Sees the Yellow House Flooded
AI Generated

{ 19 }

Hannah Hucklebee and the Great Flood

The weatherman had been reporting for several days that there would be a storm brewing in the Gulf of Mexico. Hannah and her family had been listening to the weather report and people had been talking about it at church. The forecast was calling for a hurricane to form in the Gulf, then travel up through the west side of Florida then hit Georgia, South Carolina and North Carolina as it headed on a northwesterly tract toward Tennessee.

Hannah was not very concerned because a hurricane had never reached her town of Old Fort, North Carolina. All the elders at church did not seem to be concerned but she had heard one of them say, "Boy, we could get some flooding if it does reach us. It has been raining steady for the past four days."

Often, the men at church would sit around talking about the weather and their farms or work places. Hannah liked to hear their conversations since her own father had passed away. The men at church reminded her of her daddy and hearing them talk made Hannah feel as if her dad was still around. Their laughter filled the air as they would joke and kid with one another. But when times were hard these men would join together to help anyone in trouble.

Old Fort, North Carolina lies at the foot of the Blue Ridge Mountains and just off of Interstate 40. As you drive down the highway you can see the town from the interstate bridge that crosses the main street through town. It also sits between the Catawba River and Mill

Creek that join just past the elementary school. It is home to some of the most beautiful scenery and kind people in the United States. Visitors would visit the small town for hiking and bicycling, and although changes were inevitable, it always kept its southern, country charm.

The storm was expected to hit Old Fort on Thursday of this week. Businesses were preparing for the worst but thinking all would be well. They had flooded after all, in the past, but nothing could prepare them for the devastation that was lurking just around the corner.

Hannah's mom, Martha, was a local school teacher at Old Fort Elementary School. The school was preparing for dismissal if the flood waters rose too much. Mill Creek flows just behind the school playground. Hannah and all the kids at school loved to hear the water trickling by or at times would wade in the creek barefooted. Today the water had already risen due to the rain from the past week. But no one expected what would happen on Thursday night.

Hannah, her siblings and mother were home by early evening. As light faded for the day, warnings began playing on the television. The weatherman was reporting large amounts of rain to fall for the next twenty four hours. Hannah's mom began checking for supplies in the refrigerator and for candles or oil lamps if the lights went out. Flashlight batteries were checked by her brothers, Teddy and Chester. The girls all helped check for canned food and water. Mom gave each of the children tasks to keep them from worrying. She was worrying enough for all of them. Bill, Freddie's father and Hannah's uncle called to ask if they needed anything. He had already checked on his parents, Hannah's grandparents.

The wind was picking up more and more throughout the early morning. You could hear crashing and the earth shake as big trees were uprooted. A loud bang and flash of light came from outside as a transformer blew and the power suddenly went out. In the darkness the four sisters screamed. Mom grabbed flashlights, and in a few moments, soft light covered the room. the wind howled outside and the rain poured down from the sky. Several more trees fell nearby. Mom had all the children start praying for safety from the storms. Hannah could hear her mom asking God to keep the trees away from the house. They all knelt at their mom's bedside seeking protection.

No one slept that night. Everyone was listening to the storm into the early morning. Near noon the next day the storm gradually moved away leaving a trail of destruction in it's path. Power was still off to the house and no one around them had power. Water rushed down the driveway and into the basement. Parts of the hill beside the driveway had slid into the front yard with trees and debris. Trees were down across the driveway. The neighbors were yelling back and forth to see if everyone was okay. Fortunately, on this street everyone had made it through the storm all right but, in town it was a different story.

Hannah, her mom and the other siblings were finally able to make it to Old Fort three days later. Or at least what was left of Old Fort. The rain that fell was estimated to be from 12 to 31 inches in the mountains of North Carolina and Tennessee. The mountains had acted as a funnel to pour large amounts of rain run off into already overloaded streams and rivers. All of this ran into the Catawba River, Mill Creek and Curtis Creek at the eastern end of Old Fort. This made the water current so fierce that houses, trailers, cars, animals and school buses were lifted up and moved down stream. Many homes and businesses below the railroad track, that ran through the upper part of town, were washed from it's original foundation. Some older buildings were able to stand firm, but were so full of mud and debris they were unable to open any longer. Old Fort Elementary School was flooded and all the school supplies were destroyed. The playground was gone. A school bus lay in the rubble.

Gone was the museum, the churches, the antique shop, the arts and craft gallery not to mention restaurants. And the big yellow house that everyone noticed in town was washed away. It had been the museum office but now was crushed against trees barely recognizable. Two entire trailer parks were gone. And that was in town, not the damage in the countryside. bridges were washed away and roads gone.

As they drove through town Hannah looked at the house where her daddy had gotten coal to burn one winter. It was flooded. Hannah's teacher, Mrs. Hunt's house was covered in mud and debris. Tears fell from the children's faces as mom tried to take it all in. Slowly down the mud covered street they drove. The resident's all appeared to be in shock but trying to salvage some of their personal belongings.

Hannah looked at her mother as tears ran down her mother's face. Although the school had been destroyed, their lives had been spared. Other families were not as fortunate. Hannah had heard that her aunts' sister and husband had drowned in a nearby county. Other stories circulated of entire families being lost to the massive flooding and landslides who had no time to get to safety. Everything had been lost for some as the rivers had broken free of their boundaries and washed hopes and dreams away.

Hannah and the entire family met with others at their church hoping to make sense of the storm. Plans were created to house those who had lost homes. Supplies began pouring in from around the county from families who had survived the storm. It was if a big bottle of love and compassion had been opened up and poured out on the town. Help from around the United States poured in after learning of their plight.

Hannah was amazed at the generosity of people whom they had never met. All efforts to help were much appreciated. Television stations covered the stories of so many families who had been uprooted by the hurricane. At least for a while. Local stations continued to carry the flood news but larger stations went on to the next news worthy subject. The little town of Old Fort was now out of the limelight.

Five months after the hurricane came roaring through, Hannah and her mother drove through the small town to go to the grocery store. The lower street was empty. The few businesses that could open had opened but to no tourists. There were other places to see than a town ravaged by a flood. The yellow house remained where it had been crushed. Homes that were filled with mud and water were now gutted with windows removed. Old homes that used to be so beautiful and elegant were now sitting lonely like an elder that had be forgotten. And the school remained closed. All of the students were being bussed to a neighboring school along with the teachers.

Hannah noticed a man shoveling dirt from the sidewalk in front of the arts and craft gallery along with a boy sweeping up dirt. So much dirt. So much pain. But so much determination. This was the way of country people, often called hillbillies or rednecks, pressing on despite the odds.

Hannah's heart ached to help. But what could one little girl do? Maybe one day she would write a story for her hometown of Old Fort, North Carolina. She prayed that others would never forget Old Fort, the quiet little town at the foot of the mountain. At least Hannah and others like her would always have their memories.

{ 49 } ~ BARBARA F BARNETT

Barbara Barnett is a retired nurse having worked for the past thirty years in healthcare. Married for the past twenty five years to her wonderful husband Jack, they now live in Lenoir, North Carolina. She is one of six children who grew up in the small town of Old Fort, North Carolina at the foot of the Blue Ridge Mountains. Proud does not express how she feels of her three adult children, their spouses and now ten grandchildren. She enjoys music, art, crocheting and writing. Her love of Jesus Christ has grown more throughout the years. She is an active member of Union Grove Baptist Church in Lenoir and enjoys singing in the choir. She has recently been active in volunteering with relief efforts after Hurricane Helene tore through Western North Carolina and other states on September 27, 2024 especially devastating her hometown of Old Fort. She hopes you enjoy these modified stories based on events that happened in her childhood in the 1960's and 1970's. **To God be all the glory.**

The Author (Center-White hair) With Her Five Siblings

Acknowledgements and Citations

Bibliographic details for "The Monkees"

- Page Name: The Monkees
- Author: Wikipedia Contributors
- Publisher: Wikipedia, The Free Encyclopedia.
- Date of last revision: 8 January 2025 02:30 UTC
- Date retrieved: 17 January 2025 03:08 UTC
- Permanent link: https://en.wikipedia.org/w/index.php?title=The Monkees&oldid=1268081725
- Primary contributors: revision history statistics
- Page Version ID: 1268081725

Bibliographic details for "The Wild Wild West"

- Page name: The Wild Wild West
- Author: Wikipedia contributors
- Publisher: Wikipedia, The Free Encyclopedia
- Date of last revision: 8December 2024 22:16 UTC
- Date retrieved: 17 January 2025 03:12 UTC
- Permanent link: htpp://wikipedia.org/w/index.php?title=The Wild Wild West&oldid=1261960543
- Primary contributors: revision history statistics
- Page Version ID: 1261960543

Bibliographic details for "Hurricane Helene"

- Page name: Hurricane Helene
- Author: Wikipedia contributors
- Publisher: Wikipedia, The Free Encyclopedia
- Date of the last revision: 13 January 2025 13:37 UTC
- Date retrieved: 17 January 2025 03:17 UTC
- Permanent link: https://en.wikipedia.org/w/index.php?title=Hurricane Helene&oldid=1269190931
- Primary Contributors: revision history statistics
- Page Version ID: 1269190931

Bibliographic details for "Old Fort, North Carolina"

- Page Name: Old Fort North Carolina Travel Guide
- Author: Larry Beane Co-owner Blue Ridge Mountain Life
- Publisher: Blue Ridge Mountain Life
- Date Retrieved: January 16,2025 10:42 PM EST
- Permanent Link: http://blueridgemountainlife.old-fort-nc/

Bibliographic details for "Lone Ranger"

- Page name: Lone Ranger
- Author: Wikipedia contributors
- Publisher: Wikipedia, The Free Encyclopedia
- Date of last revision: 15 January 2025 19:25 UTC
- Date retrieved: 17 January 2025 04:53 UTC
- Permanent link: https://en.wikipedia.org/w/index.php?title=Lone Ranger&oldid=1269660355
- Primary contributors: revision history statistics
- Page Version ID: 1269660355

ACKNOWLEDGEMENTS AND CITATIONS

All images used in this book have been developed using:

- https://openart.ai/wiki/after-image-creation/content-policy--commercial-use#grab-a-stamp

ACKNOWLEDGEMENTS AND CITATIONS

ACKNOWLEDGEMENTS AND CITATIONS ~ { 56 }

www.ingramcontent.com/pod-product-compliance
Lightning Source LLC
LaVergne TN
LVHW010712090325
805246LV00001B/15